Exploring the Forest

Level 8 – Purple

Helpful Hints for Reading at Home

The graphemes (written letters) and phonemes (units of sound) used throughout this series are aligned with Letters and Sounds. This offers a consistent approach to learning whether reading at home or in the classroom.

HERE IS A LIST OF PHONEMES FOR THIS PHASE OF LEARNING. AN EXAMPLE OF THE PRONUNCIATION CAN BE FOUND IN BRACKETS.

Phase 5			
ay (day)	ou (out)	ie (tie)	ea (eat)
oy (boy)	ir (girl)	ue (blue)	aw (saw)
wh (when)	ph (photo)	ew (new)	oe (toe)
au (Paul)	a_e (make)	e_e (these)	i_e (like)
o_e (home)	u_e (rule, cube)		

Phase 5 Alternative Pronunciations of Graphemes			
a (hat, what)	e (bed, she)	i (fin, find)	o (hot, so, other)
u (but, unit)	c (cat, cent)	g (got, giant)	ow (cow, blow)
ie (tied, field)	ea (eat, bread)	er (farmer, herb)	ch (chin, school, chef)
y (yes, by, very)	ou (out, shoulder, could, you)		

HERE ARE SOME WORDS WHICH YOUR CHILD MAY FIND TRICKY.

Phase 5 Tricky Words			
oh	their	people	Mr
Mrs	looked	called	asked
could			

TOP TIPS FOR HELPING YOUR CHILD TO READ:

• Allow children time to break down unfamiliar words into units of sound and then encourage children to string these sounds together to create the word.

• Encourage your child to point out any focus phonics when they are used.

• Read through the book more than once to grow confidence.

• Ask simple questions about the text to assess understanding.

• Encourage children to use illustrations as prompts.

This book focuses on the alternative pronunciations of the grapheme /ou/ and is a Purple level 8 book band.

How many things can you think of that you might find in a forest?

There are lots of different animals and plants that can be found in the forest. Depending on where you are, you will find different animals and different plants growing there.

We should always be careful exploring the forest. Some animals can be dangerous if they are surprised. So, try not to make too many sounds.

Animals might be protecting their young.

Big creatures such as deer, bears and badgers can be found in different forests around the world. Which big animals can be found in the forest near you?

Big animals leave bigger droppings that are easier to find. Fresh animal poo means that the animal is probably still nearby. You can learn a lot from animal poo.

Don't touch!

When exploring the forest, you should try looking up! Lots of forest creatures are tree-dwellers. You could find monkeys, rodents or felines up there.

Squirrels can be found in most forests because they are tree-dwelling animals. They have bushy tails and eat nuts and seeds.

Squirrels bury nuts to save them for the winter.

A good place to look for animals is near water.
Animals go to streams to drink and look for
food. Some animals live in, or near, the water.

Don't make any sounds.
You could scare the animals away.

Amphibians are animals that can be found both in and out of the water. These include toads, frogs and salamanders. Amphibians mostly eat insects and spiders.

What sound does a frog make?

Some forest creatures mostly eat plants and some mostly eat meat. There is lots to eat in the forest if you mostly eat plants.

The koala can be found in the forests of Australia.

Trees can come in all different sizes. Some are really tall with lots of branches. Some are small and leafy. Trees can also be very old.

Some trees are hundreds of years old!

There are some things that all trees have. All trees have roots that grow underground. They also all have a trunk, which is the main body of the tree.

If you see a slime mould on a tree, do not touch it.

If you are going to go up trees, make sure that you have good boots with good grip. Trees can be fun to play in, but make sure that you are careful.

©2022 BookLife Publishing Ltd.
King's Lynn, Norfolk, PE30 4LS, UK

ISBN 978-1-80155-814-3

Exploring the Forest
Written by Robin Twiddy
Designed by Drue Rintoul

An Introduction to BookLife Readers...

Our Readers have been specifically created in line with the London Institute of Education's approach to book banding and are phonetically decodable and ordered to support each phase of the Letters and Sounds document.

Each book has been created to provide the best possible reading and learning experience. Our aim is to share our love of books with children, providing both emerging readers and prolific page-turners with beautiful books that are guaranteed to provoke interest and learning, regardless of ability.

BOOK BAND GRADED using the Institute of Education's approach to levelling.

PHONETICALLY DECODABLE supporting each phase of Letters and Sounds.

EXERCISES AND QUESTIONS to offer reinforcement and to ascertain comprehension.

CLEAR DESIGN to inspire and provoke engagement, providing the reader with clear visual representations of each non-fiction topic.

AUTHOR INSIGHT:
ROBIN TWIDDY

Robin Twiddy is one of BookLife Publishing's most creative and prolific editorial talents, who imbues all his copy with a sense of adventure and energy. Robin's Cambridge-based first class honours degree in psychosocial studies offers a unique viewpoint on factual information and allows him to relay information in a manner that readers of any age are guaranteed to retain. He also holds a certificate in Teaching in the Lifelong Sector, and a post graduate certificate in Consumer Psychology.

A father of two, Robin has written many titles for BookLife and specialises in conceptual, role-playing narratives which promote interaction with the reader and inspire even the most reluctant of readers to fully engage with his books.

This book focuses on the alternative pronunciations of the grapheme /ou/ and is a Purple level 8 book band.

Image Credits Images are courtesy of Shutterstock.com. With thanks to Getty Images, Thinkstock Photo and iStockphoto. Cover – Gelpi, Abbie Warnock–Matthews, HappyPictures, Tarikdiz. p3 – kpboonjit, Tsekhmister, Hurst Photo. p4–5 – Dajahof, anastasiya adamovich. p6–7 – Dreame Walker, Valsib. p8–9 – manfredstutz, USBFCO. p10–11 – Zmrzlinar, Fauzan Maududdin. p12–13 – nattanan726, RHIMAGE. p14 – Gertjan Hooijer, Maryana Serdynska.